BREAD MACHINE RECIPES

Publications International, Ltd.
Favorite Brand Name Recipes at www.fbnr.com

Louis Weber, CEO
Publications International, Ltd.
7373 North Cicero Avenue
Lincolnwood, Illinois 60712

Front cover photography and photography on pages 15, 19 and 43 by Sanders Studios, Inc.

Photographer: Kathy Sanders
Photographer's Assistant: Scott Olson
Food Stylist: Teri Rys-Maki

Pictured on the front and back covers (*clockwise from top right*): Light Rye Rolls (*page 49*), Old-Fashioned Cinnamon Braid (*page 42*), Orange Breakfast Loaf (*page 18*), Breadsticks (*page 52*), Fresh Tomato Pizza (*page 66*), Peppered Cheese Baguettes (*page 48*) and Carrot-Raisin-Nut Bread (*page 10*).

ISBN: 0-7853-3865-9

Manufactured in U.S.A.

8 7 6 5 4 3 2 1

Contents

Bread Machine Basics 6

Loafing Around 10

Shape It Up! 40

Let's Make Pizza 66

Index 92

Acknowledgments 94

Bread Machine Basics

Remember when Grandma would make homemade bread? You could smell the dough baking throughout the house. The kitchen was all warm and toasty, and that smell . . . mmmm—you could taste the bread before it was even out of the oven.

Now imagine that homebaked goodness without all the toil your grandma went through. Making loaves of bread is as easy as pressing a button—and it's not difficult to make shaped breads or pizza doughs. Everything you make will taste just like it came from Grandma's house.

Before starting, read the manufacturer's instructions as all bread machines are slightly different. But, no matter what bread machine you use, there are a few basics to keep in mind.

Measuring Ingredients

It is important to measure ingredients carefully no matter what you're baking, but it's even more important when using a bread machine. Since all you do is add the ingredients and turn on the machine, you don't have a second chance to knead in a little more flour or add more liquid to correct mistakes. An error can't be caught until the bread is done—and then it is too late to fix it. Yeast is the most important ingredient in yeast breads; so, it is very important to measure it accurately. If there is too much yeast, the dough will over-rise, leaving an open, uneven texture and a strong yeasty flavor. If there is too little yeast, the dough will not rise enough, resulting in a dense, heavy, compact loaf.

Adding Ingredients

Follow the manufacturer's instructions for the proper order to add ingredients. Some bread machines require dry ingredients to be added first while others require liquids to be added first. If you don't follow your manufacturer's recommendations, your bread may be unsatisfactory. To be sure that you don't omit any ingredients, assemble all your ingredients on the counter in the order recommended by the owner's manual.

Except for dairy products like milk and eggs, ingredients should be added at room temperature.

What size is your bread machine?

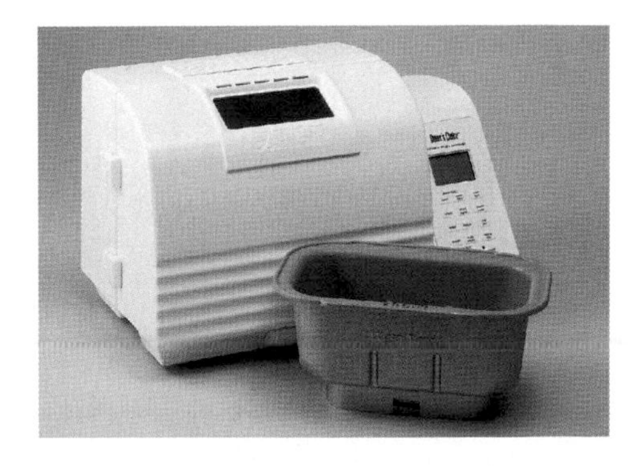

You should know the size of your bread machine before making a loaf of bread. If you are unsure, check the manual or determine the size by measuring how much water the bread pan can hold. A 1½-pound machine can hold about 12 cups of water and a 2-pound bread machine can hold about 13 to 15 cups of water. You can always make a loaf of bread that is smaller than the bread machine's capacity, but you can never make a loaf larger than the bread machine's capacity.

Once you know the size of your bread machine, you also need to know what size loaf the recipe makes. If it is not stated in the recipe, use this rule of thumb: a 1½-pound loaf calls for about 3 cups of flour while a 2-pound loaf calls for about 4 cups of flour.

When simply making dough, any size bread machine can be used.

Working with dough

When shaping dough into loaves, rolls, breadsticks or whatever you desire, there are a few basic techniques that will help to make this process much easier.

1. Sprinkle a countertop or cutting board with 1 to 2 tablespoons of flour. Place the dough on the floured surface and begin to shape. This will help keep the dough from sticking to the surface.

2. Always be sure your hands are free from soap, oils and other particles which could interfere with the flavor and texture of the bread.

3. When working with a sticky dough, flour your hands lightly to make shaping easier.

4. If, while shaping the dough, it tends to shrink and not stretch to the desired shape, cover it with a towel and let it rest a few minutes before continuing.

Keeping bread fresh

Once you make delicious bread, you want to keep it tasting like the first day you made it. To do that, follow the tips below.

1. After the bread has cooled completely, wrap it tightly in plastic wrap or place in a plastic bag or covered container.

2. Do not store in the refrigerator as this will cause the bread to dry out more quickly.

3. In hot, humid weather, bread keeps best if stored in the freezer.

4. Breads made with fats, fruit or honey stay moist longer than those made without.

How to freeze bread

If you find yourself with more bread than you can eat, freeze it for future use.

1. Slice the bread and wrap tightly in plastic wrap or place in a plastic bag or freezer container.

Slicing the bread before freezing allows you to pull out the number of slices desired without having to thaw the entire loaf.

2. To thaw bread, microwave at High for 15 seconds or wrap tightly in foil and place it in a preheated 400°F oven for about 10 minutes.

Loafing Around

Carrot-Raisin-Nut Bread

1½-POUND LOAF	2-POUND LOAF
1 cup water	1¼ cups water
1 cup shredded carrots	1½ cups shredded carrots
2 tablespoons honey	3 tablespoons honey
1½ teaspoons salt	2 teaspoons salt
2 tablespoons butter or margarine	3 tablespoons butter or margarine
3 cups bread flour	4 cups bread flour
¼ cup whole wheat flour	⅓ cup whole wheat flour
1½ teaspoons rapid-rise yeast	2 teaspoons rapid-rise yeast
⅓ cup chopped walnuts	½ cup chopped walnuts
⅓ cup raisins	½ cup raisins

1. Measure carefully, placing all ingredients except walnuts and raisins in bread machine pan in order specified by owner's manual.

2. Program basic cycle and desired crust setting; press start. Add walnuts and raisins when bread machine signals or at the end of first kneading cycle. Remove baked bread from pan; cool on wire rack.

Makes 12 or 16 servings

Carrot-Raisin-Nut Bread

Sun-Dried Tomato and Basil Bread

1½-POUND LOAF

- 1 cup water
- 1½ tablespoons sugar
- 1½ teaspoons salt
- 2 teaspoons dried basil leaves
- 2 tablespoons olive oil
- 2 tablespoons toasted wheat germ
- 2¾ cups bread flour
- ¼ cup whole wheat flour
- 1½ teaspoons rapid-rise yeast
- ¼ cup oil-packed sun-dried tomatoes, drained and chopped

2-POUND LOAF

- 1½ cups water
- 2 tablespoons sugar
- 2 teaspoons salt
- 1 tablespoon dried basil leaves
- 3 tablespoons olive oil
- 3 tablespoons toasted wheat germ
- 3½ cups bread flour
- ½ cup whole wheat flour
- 2 teaspoons rapid-rise yeast
- ⅓ cup oil-packed sun-dried tomatoes, drained and chopped

1. Measure carefully, placing all ingredients except tomatoes in bread machine pan in order specified by owner's manual. Spoon tomatoes into 4 corners of pan; do not cover yeast.

2. Program basic cycle and desired crust setting; press start. Remove baked bread from pan; cool on wire rack. *Makes 12 or 16 servings*

Sun-Dried Tomato and Basil Bread

Apricot Holiday Bread

INGREDIENTS

⅔ cup milk
1 teaspoon salt
1 egg
2 tablespoons butter or margarine, softened
3 cups all-purpose flour
2 tablespoons sugar
1 tablespoon active dry yeast
½ cup pecan or walnut pieces
½ cup dried apricots or peaches, chopped
¼ teaspoon ground ginger
¼ teaspoon ground nutmeg

1. Measure carefully, placing all ingredients in bread machine pan in order specified by owner's manual.

2. Program basic or white cycle and desired crust setting; press start. *(Do not use delay cycles.)* Remove baked bread from pan; cool on wire rack.

Makes 1 (1½-pound) loaf

Basic Yeast Bread

INGREDIENTS

1 cup milk
1 teaspoon salt
1 egg
2 tablespoons unsalted butter, softened
3¼ cups all-purpose bread flour
1 tablespoon sugar
2 teaspoons active dry yeast

1. Measure carefully, placing all ingredients in bread machine pan in order specified by owner's manual.

2. Program basic or white cycle and desired crust setting; press start.* *(Do not use delay cycles.)* Remove baked bread from pan; cool on wire rack.

Makes 1 (1½-pound) loaf

*When making Basic Yeast Bread dough, follow recipe through step 1. Program dough cycle setting; press start.

Apricot Holiday Bread

Gannat (French Cheese Bread)

INGREDIENTS

- 3 tablespoons water
- 1 teaspoon salt
- 2 eggs
- ¼ cup butter or margarine, cut up, softened
- 2½ cups all-purpose flour
- 1 teaspoon sugar
- 1 cup (4 ounces) shredded Cheddar or Swiss cheese
- 2 teaspoons active dry yeast

1. Measure carefully, placing all ingredients in bread machine pan in order specified by owner's manual.

2. Program basic or white cycle and desired crust setting; press start. *(Do not use delay cycles.)* Remove baked bread from pan; cool on wire rack.

Makes 1 (1½-pound) loaf

Honey of a Whole Wheat Bread

1-POUND LOAF

- 1½ teaspoons RED STAR® Active Dry Yeast
- 1⅓ cups bread flour
- ⅔ cup whole wheat flour
- 1½ teaspoons salt
- 2 teaspoons butter, cut into small pieces
- 2 tablespoons honey (80°F)
- ¼ cup milk (80°F)
- ¼ cup water (80°F)
- 1 large egg, at room temperature

1½-POUND LOAF

- 2¼ teaspoons RED STAR® Active Dry Yeast
- 2 cups bread flour
- 1 cup whole wheat flour
- 2 teaspoons salt
- 1 tablespoon butter, cut into small pieces
- ¼ cup honey (80°F)
- ½ cup milk (80°F)
- ¼ cup water (80°F)
- 1 large egg, at room temperature

Place ingredients into pan in order specified by bread machine owner's manual. Set bread machine on basic/standard bread-making setting; select medium or normal baking cycle. Cool bread to room temperature before slicing.

Makes 1 loaf

Jalapeño Cheese Bread

1-POUND LOAF

⅔ cup water
1 tablespoon plus 1 teaspoon margarine, softened
2 cups bread flour
¼ cup nonfat dry milk
2 teaspoons sugar
¾ teaspoon salt
½ cup shredded Cheddar cheese
1 tablespoon diced and seeded jalapeño peppers
1¼ teaspoons active dry yeast

1½-POUND LOAF

1 cup water
2 tablespoons margarine, softened
3 cups bread flour
⅓ cup nonfat dry milk
1 tablespoon sugar
1 teaspoon salt
⅔ cup shredded Cheddar cheese
1½ tablespoons diced and seeded jalapeño peppers
2 teaspoons active dry yeast

2-POUND LOAF

1⅓ cups water
2 tablespoons plus 2 teaspoons margarine, softened
4 cups bread flour
½ cup nonfat dry milk
1 tablespoon plus 1 teaspoon sugar
1½ teaspoons salt
1 cup shredded Cheddar cheese
2 tablespoons diced and seeded jalapeño peppers
2½ teaspoons active dry yeast

1. Measure carefully, placing all ingredients in bread machine pan in order specified by owner's manual.

2. Program desired cycle; press start. *(Do not use delay cycles.)* Remove baked bread from pan; cool on wire rack. *Makes 1 loaf*

Favorite recipe from *North Dakota Wheat Commission*

Crusty Rye Bread

INGREDIENTS

1 cup water
1 teaspoon salt
1 tablespoon butter or margarine, softened
2½ cups all-purpose flour
½ cup rye flour
¼ cup packed light brown sugar
3 strips pared orange peel, chopped
1 teaspoon caraway seeds
2 teaspoons active dry yeast

1. Measure carefully, placing all ingredients in bread machine pan in order specified by owner's manual.

2. Program basic or white cycle and desired crust setting; press start. Remove baked bread from pan; cool. *Makes 1 (1½-pound) loaf*

Orange Breakfast Loaf

INGREDIENTS

1 cup water
1 teaspoon salt
⅓ cup orange juice
2 tablespoons vegetable oil
2 tablespoons sugar
1 cup oats
1 cup whole wheat flour
2 cups all-purpose flour
1 teaspoon grated orange peel
½ cup dried cranberries
2 teaspoons active dry yeast

1. Measure carefully, placing all ingredients in bread machine pan in order specified by owner's manual.

2. Program basic or white cycle and desired crust setting; press start. Remove baked bread from pan; cool. *Makes 1 (1½-pound) loaf*

Crusty Rye Bread

Oatmeal-Raisin Bread

1½-POUND LOAF	2-POUND LOAF
1¼ cups water	1½ cups water
¼ cup nonfat dry milk	⅓ cup nonfat dry milk
2 tablespoons honey	3 tablespoons honey
1 tablespoon margarine or butter	2 tablespoons margarine or butter
1½ teaspoons salt	2 teaspoons salt
3 cups bread flour	4 cups bread flour
1½ teaspoons rapid-rise yeast	2 teaspoons rapid-rise yeast
½ cup old-fashioned oats	¾ cup old-fashioned oats
½ cup raisins	¾ cup raisins

1. Measure carefully, placing all ingredients except oats and raisins in bread machine pan in order specified by owner's manual.

2. Program basic cycle and desired crust setting; press start. Add oats and raisins at the beep or at the end of first kneading cycle. Remove baked bread from pan; cool on wire rack. *Makes 12 or 16 servings*

Old-Fashioned Hearth Bread

INGREDIENTS

- ¾ cup water
- 1 teaspoon salt
- 1 tablespoon butter or margarine, softened
- 2 tablespoons honey or light molasses
- 2 cups all-purpose flour
- 2 tablespoons instant nonfat dry milk solids
- 1 tablespoon wheat germ
- 2 teaspoons active dry yeast

1. Measure carefully, placing all ingredients in bread machine pan in order specified by owner's manual.

2. Program basic or white cycle and desired crust setting; press start. Remove baked bread from pan; cool. *Makes 1 (1½-pound) loaf*

Oatmeal-Raisin Bread

Jalapeño Corn Bread

1½-POUND LOAF	2-POUND LOAF
¾ cup plus 1 tablespoon water	1 cup plus 2 tablespoons water
1 cup thawed frozen or drained canned corn	1½ cups thawed frozen or drained canned corn
1 tablespoon buttermilk powder	2 tablespoons buttermilk powder
1 tablespoon minced drained bottled jalapeño peppers*	2 tablespoons minced drained bottled jalapeño peppers*
1½ teaspoons salt	2 teaspoons salt
1 tablespoon sugar	2 tablespoons sugar
¾ cup cornmeal	1 cup cornmeal
2¾ cups bread flour	3½ cups bread flour
1 cup shredded Monterey Jack cheese	1½ cups shredded Monterey Jack cheese
1 teaspoon rapid-rise yeast	1½ teaspoons rapid-rise yeast

*For less spicy bread, use 1 to 2 teaspoons jalapeño peppers. Jalapeño peppers can sting and irritate the skin; wear rubber gloves when handling peppers and do not touch eyes.

1. Measure carefully, placing all ingredients in bread machine pan in order specified by owner's manual.

2. Program basic or white cycle and desired crust setting; press start. Remove baked bread from pan; cool on wire rack

Makes 12 or 16 servings

Jalapeño Corn Bread

Maple-Walnut Bread

1½-POUND LOAF	2-POUND LOAF
1¼ cups water	1½ cups water
¼ cup maple or pancake syrup	⅓ cup maple or pancake syrup
¼ teaspoon maple extract	½ teaspoon maple extract
1½ teaspoons salt	2 teaspoons salt
½ teaspoon ground cinnamon	¾ teaspoon ground cinnamon
1 tablespoon butter	2 tablespoons butter
3 cups bread flour	4 cups bread flour
¼ cup whole wheat flour	⅓ cup whole wheat flour
½ cup coarsely chopped walnuts	¾ cup coarsely chopped walnuts
1½ teaspoons rapid-rise yeast	2 teaspoons rapid-rise yeast

1. Measure carefully, placing all ingredients in bread machine pan in order specified by owner's manual.

2. Program basic or white cycle and desired crust setting; press start. Remove baked bread from pan; cool on wire rack.

Makes 12 or 16 servings

Maple-Walnut Bread

Parmesan and Herb Bread

1-POUND LOAF

- ¾ cup water
- 2 teaspoons oil
- 2 cups bread flour
- ¼ cup grated Parmesan cheese
- 1 tablespoon nonfat dry milk
- 1 tablespoon sugar
- 1 tablespoon plus 1 teaspoon Italian herb seasoning
- ¾ teaspoon salt
- ¼ teaspoon garlic powder
- 1½ teaspoons active dry yeast

1½-POUND LOAF

- 1 cup plus 2 tablespoons water
- 1 tablespoon oil
- 3 cups bread flour
- ⅓ cup grated Parmesan cheese
- 1½ tablespoons nonfat dry milk
- 1½ tablespoons sugar
- 2 tablespoons Italian herb seasoning
- 1¼ teaspoons salt
- ½ teaspoon garlic powder
- 2 teaspoons active dry yeast

2-POUND LOAF

- 1½ cups water
- 1 tablespoon plus 1 teaspoon oil
- 4 cups bread flour
- ½ cup grated Parmesan cheese
- 2 tablespoons nonfat dry milk
- 2 tablespoons sugar
- 2½ tablespoons Italian herb seasoning
- 1½ teaspoons salt
- ¾ teaspoon garlic powder
- 1 tablespoon active dry yeast

1. Measure carefully, placing all ingredients in bread machine pan in order specified by owner's manual.

2. Program desired cycle; press start. *(Do not use delay cycles.)* Remove baked bread from pan; cool on wire rack. *Makes 1 loaf*

Favorite recipe from *North Dakota Wheat Commission*

Cracked Wheat Bread

1-POUND LOAF

- **¾ cup plus 2 tablespoons water**
- **½ cup cracked wheat**
- **1 tablespoon plus 1 teaspoon margarine**
- **1 tablespoon plus 1 teaspoon honey**
- **2¼ cups bread flour**
- **1 teaspoon salt**
- **1½ teaspoons active dry yeast**

1½-POUND LOAF

- **1¼ cups plus 1 tablespoon water**
- **¾ cup cracked wheat**
- **2 tablespoons margarine**
- **2 tablespoons honey**
- **3 cups bread flour**
- **1½ teaspoons salt**
- **2¼ teaspoons active dry yeast**

2-POUND LOAF

- **1¾ cup water**
- **1 cup cracked wheat**
- **2 tablespoons plus 2 teaspoons margarine**
- **3 tablespoons honey**
- **4 cups bread flour**
- **2 teaspoons salt**
- **1 tablespoon active dry yeast**

1. Bring water to a boil. In small bowl, pour water over cracked wheat and let cool until 80°F.

2. Measure carefully, placing remaining ingredients and cracked wheat in bread machine pan in order specified by owner's manual.

3. Program desired cycle; press start. Remove baked bread from pan; cool on wire rack. *Makes 1 loaf*

Favorite recipe from *North Dakota Wheat Commission*

Potato Bread

1½-POUND LOAF	2-POUND LOAF
1⅓ cups water	**1¾ cups water**
1½ tablespoons margarine or butter	**2 tablespoons margarine or butter**
2 tablespoons sugar	**3 tablespoons sugar**
2 tablespoons nonfat dry milk	**3 tablespoons nonfat dry milk**
1½ teaspoons salt	**2 teaspoons salt**
3 cups bread flour	**4 cups bread flour**
½ cup mashed potato flakes	**¾ cup mashed potato flakes**
1½ teaspoons rapid-rise yeast	**2 teaspoons rapid-rise yeast**

1. Measure carefully, placing all ingredients in bread machine pan in order specified by owner's manual.

2. Program basic cycle and desired crust setting; press start. Remove baked bread from pan; cool on wire rack. *Makes 12 or 16 servings*

Serving Suggestion: Serve with an herb butter. Stir together ½ cup softened butter and 1 tablespoon of your favorite herbs.

Potato Bread

German Rye Beer Bread

1½-POUND LOAF	2-POUND LOAF
1¼ cups room temperature beer	**1½ cups room temperature beer**
2 tablespoons light molasses	**3 tablespoons light molasses**
1 tablespoon butter	**1½ tablespoons butter**
1½ teaspoons salt	**2 teaspoons salt**
2 teaspoons caraway seeds	**1 tablespoon caraway seeds**
2½ cups bread flour	**3¼ cups bread flour**
½ cup rye flour	**¾ cup rye flour**
1½ teaspoons rapid-rise yeast	**2 teaspoons rapid-rise yeast**

1. Measure carefully, placing all ingredients in bread machine pan in order specified by owner's manual. Program basic cycle and desired crust setting; press start. Remove baked bread from pan; cool on wire rack.

Makes 12 or 16 servings

Cherry Granola Bread

INGREDIENTS

2½ teaspoons active dry yeast
2 cups bread flour
1¼ cups whole wheat flour
3 tablespoons nonfat dry milk powder
1½ teaspoons salt
1¼ cups water
2 tablespoons honey
2 tablespoons vegetable oil
⅔ cup granola
½ cup dried tart cherries

1. Measure carefully, placing all ingredients except granola and cherries in bread machine pan in order specified by owner's manual. Program desired cycle; press start. Add granola and cherries at the beep or at the end of the first kneading cycle. Remove baked bread from pan; cool on wire rack.

Makes 1 loaf (about 16 slices)

Favorite recipe from *Cherry Marketing Institute*

German Rye Beer Bread

Dakota Bread

INGREDIENTS

½ cup water
2 tablespoons sunflower oil
1 egg, beaten
½ cup cottage cheese
¼ cup honey
2 cups bread flour
½ cup whole wheat flour
¼ cup wheat germ
¼ cup rye flour
¼ cup rolled oats, quick cooking
1 teaspoon salt
1 tablespoon wheat gluten
1¼ teaspoons active dry yeast
¼ cup roasted, unsalted sunflower seeds (optional)

1. Measure carefully, placing all ingredients in bread machine pan in order specified by owner's manual.

2. Program desired cycle; press start. *(Do not use delay cycles.)* Remove baked bread from pan; cool on wire rack. *Makes 1 loaf (24 slices)*

Favorite recipe from *North Dakota Wheat Commission*

Pepper Sweet Corn Bread

INGREDIENTS

2 tablespoons oil
½ cup water
1 egg
½ cup sweet corn
1 cup chopped red bell pepper
1 teaspoon paprika
1 teaspoon salt
⅓ cup cornmeal
2 cups bread flour
1½ teaspoons RED STAR® Active Dry Yeast or QUICK•RISE™ Yeast

Bread Machine Method

Select Red Star® Active Dry Yeast or Quick•Rise™ Yeast as is appropriate for your automatic bread machine. All ingredients should be at room temperature. Place ingredients into pan in the order suggested by the machine's manual. *Makes 1 loaf*

Note: Cook sweet corn and cut off the cob.

Dilled Buttermilk Bread

1½-POUND LOAF	2-POUND LOAF
½ cup water	**¾ cup water**
1 egg, lightly beaten	**1 egg, lightly beaten**
½ cup buttermilk*	**¾ cup buttermilk***
1 tablespoon sugar	**2 tablespoons sugar**
1 tablespoon butter	**1½ tablespoons butter**
3 cups bread flour	**4 cups bread flour**
1½ teaspoons dried dill weed	**2 teaspoons dried dill weed**
1 teaspoon salt	**1½ teaspoons salt**
1½ teaspoons rapid-rise yeast	**2 teaspoons rapid-rise yeast**

*You may substitute soured fresh milk. To sour milk, place 1 tablespoon lemon juice plus enough milk to equal 1 cup in 2-cup measure. Stir; let stand 5 minutes before using.

1. Measure carefully, placing all ingredients in bread machine pan in order specified by owner's manual.

2. Program basic cycle and desired crust setting; press start. *(Do not use delay cycles.)* Remove baked bread from pan; cool on wire rack.

Makes 12 or 16 servings

Serving Suggestion: Serve with a flavored butter. Stir together ½ cup softened butter, 1 tablespoon chopped parsley and 1 tablespoon chopped red bell pepper in a small bowl.

Dilled Buttermilk Bread

Multigrain Bread

1½-POUND LOAF	2-POUND LOAF
1¼ cups boiling water	**1½ cups boiling water**
¼ cup multigrain cereal	**⅓ cup multigrain cereal**
2 tablespoons quick oats	**¼ cup quick oats**
2 tablespoons honey	**3 tablespoons honey**
1 tablespoon margarine or butter	**1½ tablespoons margarine or butter**
1 teaspoon salt	**1½ teaspoons salt**
2½ cups bread flour	**3¼ cups bread flour**
1½ teaspoons rapid-rise yeast	**2 teaspoons rapid-rise yeast**

1. Place water in bread machine pan. Add cereal and oats. Let stand 30 minutes or until cool. Measure carefully, placing remaining ingredients in bread machine pan in order specified by owner's manual.

2. Program basic cycle and desired crust setting; press start. Remove baked bread from pan; cool on wire rack. *Makes 12 or 16 servings*

Serving Suggestion: Serve with an orange-flavored butter. Stir together ½ cup softened butter and 1 tablespoon orange zest.

Multigrain Bread

Honey Wheat Bread

INGREDIENTS

½ cup water
1 teaspoon salt
1 egg
2 tablespoons butter or margarine, softened
3 tablespoons honey
2 cups all-purpose flour
¾ cup whole wheat flour
¼ cup instant nonfat dry milk solids
2 teaspoons active dry yeast

1. Measure carefully, placing all ingredients in bread machine pan in order specified by owner's manual.

2. Program basic or white cycle and desired crust setting; press start. *(Do not use delay cycles.)* Remove baked bread from pan; cool on wire rack.

Makes 1 (1-pound) loaf

Honey Wheat Bread

Shape It Up!

Hot Cross Buns

INGREDIENTS

Basic Yeast Bread (page 14)
1 cup raisins
¼ cup powdered sugar
1 to 2 tablespoons heavy cream

1. Prepare Basic Yeast Bread dough as instructed, adding raisins at the end of the first kneading cycle.

2. Grease 13×9-inch pan; set aside. Turn out dough onto lightly oiled surface. Cover with clean towel; let rest 5 minutes.

3. Divide dough into 15 equal pieces. Form each piece into ball. Place evenly spaced in prepared pan. Cover with towel; let rise in warm place 45 minutes.

4. Preheat oven to 400°F. Bake 15 minutes or until golden brown. Immediately remove from pan; cool on wire rack 30 minutes.

5. Combine powdered sugar and cream, 1 tablespoon at a time, in measuring cup. Add additional cream to reach desired consistency. Pour mixture in thin stream across each bun to form a cross.

Makes 15 buns

Hot Cross Buns

Old-Fashioned Cinnamon Braid

INGREDIENTS

1 cup water
1 teaspoon salt
¼ cup butter
3¾ cups all-purpose flour
¼ cup granulated sugar
2 teaspoons active dry yeast
Cinnamon Sugar Filling (recipe follows)
Glaze (recipe follows)

1. Measure carefully, placing all ingredients except Cinnamon Sugar Filling and Glaze in bread machine pan in order specified by owner's manual. Program dough cycle setting; press start.

2. Divide dough into 3 equal pieces. Roll each piece into 14-inch-long rope. Prepare Cinnamon Sugar Filling. Brush filling on one side of each rope. Starting from middle, braid ropes. Tuck ends under and pinch to seal. Place on greased baking sheet. Cover and let rise in warm place 45 minutes or until doubled.

3. Preheat oven to 350°F. Bake 35 to 40 minutes or until evenly browned and braid sounds hollow when tapped. Remove from baking sheet; cool on wire rack. Prepare Glaze; drizzle over braid.

Makes 1 loaf

Cinnamon Sugar Filling

¼ cup butter
¼ cup packed brown sugar
2 teaspoons ground cinnamon

1. Melt butter in small saucepan over low heat. Add sugar and cinnamon.

Glaze

3 to 4 tablespoons milk
1 cup powdered sugar

1. Whisk 3 tablespoons milk and powdered sugar together in small bowl. If Glaze is too thick, add remaining milk.

Old-Fashioned Cinnamon Braid

Caramel Sticky Buns

INGREDIENTS

½ cup water
1 teaspoon salt
1 egg, beaten
2¼ cups all-purpose flour
3 tablespoons sugar
2 tablespoons instant nonfat dry milk solids
2 teaspoons active dry yeast
Caramel Topping (recipe follows)
3 tablespoons butter or margarine, melted

1. Measure carefully, placing all ingredients except Caramel Topping and butter in bread machine pan in order specified by owner's manual. Program dough cycle; press start.

2. Prepare Caramel Topping while dough is rising. Pour topping into greased 9-inch round cake or pie pan. Turn out dough onto lightly oiled surface. Cut dough into 12 equal pieces. Shape each piece into smooth ball. Dip into melted butter; arrange over Caramel Topping in pan. Cover and let rise in warm place about 1 hour or until doubled.

3. Preheat oven to 400°F. Bake 10 to 12 minutes or until brown. Cool about 1 minute; invert onto serving plate. Serve warm or at room temperature.

Makes 12 rolls

Caramel Topping

3 tablespoons packed brown sugar
3 tablespoons butter or margarine
2 tablespoons dark corn syrup
¼ cup chopped walnuts or pecans

1. Combine brown sugar, butter and corn syrup in small saucepan. Cook over medium heat, stirring constantly, until bubbly and brown sugar dissolves. Remove from heat; stir in nuts.

Saint Lucia Crown

INGREDIENTS

¼ cup water
¼ cup milk
1 teaspoon salt
3 eggs, divided
¼ cup butter or margarine, softened
2¾ cups all-purpose flour
4 tablespoons granulated sugar
½ cup golden raisins
¼ cup chopped blanched almonds
2 teaspoons active dry yeast
1 tablespoon cold water
Sugar Icing (recipe follows)

1. Measure carefully, placing all ingredients except 1 egg, 1 tablespoon cold water and Sugar Icing in bread machine pan in order specified by owner's manual. Program dough cycle setting; press start.

2. Cut off about ⅓ cup dough; reserve. Divide remaining dough into 3 equal pieces. Shape each piece into 25-inch-long rope. Braid together and place on greased baking sheet. Twist into ring about 8 inches in diameter. Pinch ends together to seal. Shape reserved ⅓ cup dough into 12-inch-long rope. Shape into bow and place over seam of braided ring. Cover and let rise in warm place 45 minutes or until doubled.

3. Preheat oven to 350°F. Beat remaining egg with cold water. Brush over dough. Bake 25 to 30 minutes or until evenly browned. Prepare Sugar Icing while bread is baking. Remove bread from baking sheet; cool on wire rack.

4. Drizzle Sugar Icing over bread; cool. If desired, make 4 to 6 small holes in bread and insert candles into holes. *Makes 1 loaf*

Sugar Icing

1 cup powdered sugar
1 teaspoon butter, softened
2 to 3 tablespoons milk

1. Combine sugar, butter and 2 tablespoons milk in small bowl. If icing is too thick, add remaining milk.

Chocolate Rolls

INGREDIENTS

Basic Yeast Bread (page 14)
½ cup granulated sugar
3 tablespoons unsweetened cocoa powder, divided
½ teaspoon ground cinnamon
3 tablespoons butter, melted
1 cup powdered sugar
¼ to ½ cup heavy cream, divided

1. Prepare Basic Yeast Bread dough as instructed.

2. Grease 13×9-inch pan; set aside. Turn out dough onto lightly oiled work surface. Roll dough into 20×15-inch rectangle.

3. Combine granulated sugar, 2 tablespoons cocoa and cinnamon in small bowl.

4. Brush melted butter over dough, leaving ½-inch border on top short edge. Sprinkle sugar mixture over dough. Starting at short side; loosely roll up jelly-roll style. Using heavy thread or dental floss, cut dough into 12 equal slices. Place slices, cut side up, in prepared pan. Cover with towel; let rise in warm place 45 minutes.

5. Preheat oven to 375°F. Bake 20 minutes or until golden brown. Allow rolls to cool in pan 30 minutes.

6. Combine powdered sugar, remaining 1 tablespoon cocoa and 2 tablespoons cream in glass measuring cup. Add additional cream if necessary to reach desired consistency. Drizzle over tops of rolls.

Makes 12 rolls

Chocolate Rolls

Peppered Cheese Baguettes

INGREDIENTS

- **¾ cup water**
- **1½ teaspoons salt**
- **2 tablespoons butter or margarine, softened**
- **1 teaspoon red pepper sauce**
- **2¾ cups all-purpose flour**
- **⅓ cup shredded Swiss cheese**
- **2 tablespoons grated Parmesan cheese**
- **¼ teaspoon ground black pepper**
- **1 tablespoon sugar**
- **2 teaspoons active dry yeast**
- **Vegetable oil**

1. Measure carefully, placing all ingredients except oil in bread machine pan in order specified by owner's manual. Program dough cycle setting; press start.

2. Divide dough into 2 equal pieces. Roll each piece into 12-inch-long rope. Place on greased baking sheet. Cover and let rise in warm place 40 minutes or until doubled.

3. Preheat oven to 350°F. Brush dough with oil. Bake 20 to 25 minutes or until golden and loaves sound hollow when tapped. Remove from baking sheet; cool on wire rack.

Makes 2 loaves

Light Rye Rolls

INGREDIENTS

1 cup water
¾ teaspoon salt
¼ cup butter or margarine, cut into 4 pieces, softened
2½ cups all-purpose flour
½ cup rye flour
⅓ cup wheat germ
¼ cup packed light brown sugar
2 teaspoons active dry yeast
1 egg white, slightly beaten
Caraway seeds

1. Measure carefully, placing all ingredients except egg white and caraway seeds in bread machine pan in order specified by owner's manual. Program dough cycle setting; press start.

2. Turn out dough onto lightly floured surface; roll ½ inch thick. Cut dough into circles using lightly floured 2½-inch round biscuit or cookie cutter. Reroll scraps; cut into circles. Place rolls, 1½ inches apart, on greased baking sheet. Cover and let rise in warm place about 1 hour or until doubled.

3. Preheat oven to 400°F. Uncover rolls and brush with beaten egg white. Sprinkle with caraway seeds. Bake 10 to 12 minutes or until golden. Remove immediately from baking sheet; cool on wire rack.

Makes 1 dozen rolls

Savory Pull-Apart Loaves

INGREDIENTS

Basic Yeast Bread (page 14)
1 tablespoon dried basil
1 tablespoon rubbed sage
1 tablespoon dried thyme
1 tablespoon olive oil

1. Prepare Basic Yeast Bread dough as instructed.

2. Grease 9×5-inch loaf pan; set aside. Combine basil, sage and thyme in small bowl; set aside. Turn out dough onto lightly floured work surface. Divide dough into 16 equal pieces. Form each piece into ball. Cover with clean towel; let rest 5 minutes.

3. Flatten each ball into 4×3-inch oval. Coat both sides of dough with olive oil. Sprinkle one side of each dough oval with rounded ½ teaspoon herb mixture.

4. Stand loaf pan on short end. Lay one piece of dough, herb-covered side down, in pan. Stack remaining 15 pieces of dough in pan so that herb-covered sides of dough are touching sides of dough not covered with herb mixture. Cover with towel; let rise in warm place 45 minutes.

5. Preheat oven to 375°F. Bake 35 minutes or until top of loaf is golden. Immediately remove bread from pan and cool on wire rack.

Makes 1 loaf

Savory Pull-Apart Loaves

Breadsticks

12 BREADSTICKS

1¼ cups water
1 teaspoon salt
1 teaspoon sugar
1 tablespoon olive or vegetable oil
3 cups bread flour
1 tablespoon rapid-rise yeast

16 BREADSTICKS

1½ cups water
1½ teaspoons salt
1½ teaspoons sugar
2 tablespoons olive or vegetable oil
4 cups bread flour
1 tablespoon rapid-rise yeast

TOPPINGS:

2 to 3 tablespoons olive or vegetable oil
1½ to 2 tablespoons coarse salt, poppy seeds or sesame seeds

1. Measure carefully, placing all ingredients except toppings in bread machine pan in order specified by owner's manual. Program dough cycle setting; press start.

2. Turn out dough onto lightly oiled surface. Work dough into smooth ball using lightly floured hands. Cut dough into 12 pieces for small batch or 16 pieces for large batch. Roll each piece into 16-inch rope; twist rope and place on greased baking sheets.

3. Brush breadsticks with 2 to 3 tablespoons oil. Sprinkle ungreased baking sheet with salt. Roll breadsticks, 1 at a time, in salt; place back on greased baking sheets. Preheat oven to 350°F. Breadsticks will rise slightly while oven preheats. Bake 30 to 35 minutes or until golden brown and crispy. *Makes 12 or 16 breadsticks*

Greek Flat Breads

INGREDIENTS

Basic Yeast Bread (page 14)
½ cup chopped kalamata olives
3 cloves garlic, minced
¼ pound crumbled feta cheese
1 tablespoon olive oil
1 egg
1 tablespoon water
Coarse salt (optional)

1. Prepare Basic Yeast Bread dough as instructed.

2. Grease baking sheet; set aside. Turn out dough onto lightly oiled surface. Divide dough into 16 equal pieces. Form each piece into ball. Cover with clean towel; let rest 5 minutes.

3. Combine olives, garlic, cheese and oil in medium bowl; set aside. Beat egg with 1 tablespoon water.

4. Flatten each ball of dough to ½-inch thickness. Place 2 inches apart on prepared baking sheet. Brush dough with beaten egg mixture. Sprinkle each round with equal amount of olive mixture; press topping into dough slightly. Cover with towel; let rise in warm place 45 minutes.

5. Place heavy pan on lower rack of oven. Preheat oven to 400°F. Sprinkle tops of dough with coarse salt, if desired. Place bread in oven. Carefully place 4 to 5 ice cubes in heavy pan; close door immediately. Bake 15 minutes or until lightly browned. Immediately remove bread from baking sheets to wire rack; cool. *Makes 16 flat breads*

Greek Flat Breads

Buttery Pan Rolls

INGREDIENTS

¼ cup water
¼ cup cold milk
½ teaspoon salt
1 egg, beaten
8 tablespoons butter or margarine, melted and cooled, divided
2 cups all-purpose flour
2 tablespoons sugar
2 teaspoons active dry yeast

1. Measure carefully, placing all ingredients except 5 tablespoons melted butter in bread machine pan in order specified by owner's manual. Program dough cycle setting; press start.

2. Pour half of the remaining melted butter into 8-inch square baking pan. Tilt pan to completely coat bottom with butter. Drop batter by rounded tablespoonfuls into pan, making 16 rolls. Drizzle remaining melted butter over rolls. Cover loosely with plastic wrap and let rise in warm place 30 to 40 minutes or until almost doubled.

3. Preheat oven to 400°F. Uncover rolls and bake 12 to 15 minutes or until golden. Cool slightly in pan on wire rack. *Makes 16 rolls*

Cinnamon Pear Rolls

INGREDIENTS

½ cup warm water (80°F)
1 (6-ounce) jar baby food pears, divided
1 egg, lightly beaten
3 cups bread flour
3 tablespoons granulated sugar
1 tablespoon nonfat dry milk
½ teaspoon salt
1 package rapid rise yeast
⅓ cup packed brown sugar
1½ teaspoons ground cinnamon
½ cup raisins or nuts (optional)
½ cup powdered sugar
¼ teaspoon vanilla extract
1 to 2 teaspoons milk

1. Measure carefully, placing water, ½ cup pears, egg, flour, granulated sugar, dry milk, salt and yeast in bread machine pan in order specified in owner's manual, adding pears with liquids. Program dough cycle setting; press start.

2. Turn out dough onto lightly floured surface; knead until dough is easy to handle. Cover; let rest 10 minutes.

3. Roll dough into a 14×10-inch rectangle. Spread with remaining pears (about 2 tablespoons). Mix brown sugar with cinnamon and sprinkle over dough; add raisins or nuts. Roll up, beginning with long side. Pinch seam to seal. Cut roll into 12 slices and place in 13×9-inch baking pan coated with nonstick spray. Cover; let rise in warm place 45 minutes or until doubled.

4. Preheat oven to 375°F. Bake 25 to 30 minutes. Remove from pan; cool on wire rack. Mix powdered sugar, vanilla and milk to make a thin icing. Drizzle over warm rolls. *Makes 12 rolls*

Favorite recipe from *North Dakota Wheat Commission*

Bagels

6 BAGELS	9 BAGELS
1 cup plus 3 tablespoons water	1½ cups water
2 tablespoons sugar	3 tablespoons sugar
1½ teaspoons salt	2 teaspoons salt
3 cups bread flour	4 cups bread flour
2 teaspoons rapid-rise yeast	2 teaspoons rapid-rise yeast

FOR BOILING AND BAKING:

- **3 quarts water**
- **1 tablespoon sugar**
- **2 to 3 tablespoons cornmeal**
- **1 egg, beaten**
- **1 to 2 tablespoons sesame seeds, poppy seeds, caraway seeds or cinnamon sugar (optional)**

1. Measure carefully, placing all ingredients except those required for boiling and baking in bread machine pan in order specified by owner's manual. Program dough cycle setting; press start.

2. Turn out dough onto floured surface; knead briefly. Cut into 6 pieces for small batch or 9 pieces for large batch. Shape into balls. Place on floured surface; let rest 10 minutes. Poke thumb through center of each ball to make hole. Stretch into doughnut shapes. Place back on floured surface. Let rise, uncovered, 15 minutes or until puffy. Do not overproof bagels.

3. For boiling and baking, preheat oven to 400°F. Bring water and sugar to a boil in large, deep skillet or wok. Spray 2 baking sheets with nonstick cooking spray; sprinkle with cornmeal. Carefully lower bagels, 3 at a time, into boiling water. Boil 5 minutes, turning often. Remove bagels using slotted spoon; drain briefly on paper towels. Place 2 inches apart on prepared baking sheets. Brush with beaten egg and sprinkle with sesame seeds, if desired. Bake 25 to 30 minutes or until golden brown. Remove from baking sheets; cool on wire rack.

Makes 6 or 9 bagels

Italian Pan Rolls

INGREDIENTS

¾ cup warm water
1 teaspoon garlic salt
1 tablespoon cold butter or margarine
2¾ cups all-purpose flour
1 tablespoon sugar
½ teaspoon Italian herb seasoning *or* ¼ teaspoon *each* dried oregano and basil leaves
2 teaspoons active dry yeast
2 tablespoons olive oil, vegetable oil or melted butter
¼ cup grated Parmesan cheese

1. Measure carefully, placing all ingredients except olive oil and cheese in bread machine pan in order specified by owner's manual. Program dough cycle setting; press start.

2. Divide dough into quarters, then divide again into quarters, making 16 pieces. Shape each piece into smooth ball. Dip each ball in oil; coat with cheese and arrange in greased 8 or 9-inch round or square cake pan. Cover loosely with plastic wrap and let rise in warm place 1 to 1½ hours or until doubled.

3. Preheat oven to 375°F. Uncover rolls and bake 25 minutes or until golden. Remove immediately from pan; cool on wire rack.

Makes 16 rolls

Honey Pecan Coffee Cake

INGREDIENTS

½ cup water
¾ teaspoon salt
2 eggs
3 tablespoons butter or margarine, softened
2¾ cups all-purpose flour
¼ cup sugar
1 package active dry yeast
¼ cup honey
½ cup chopped pecans, toasted

1. Measure carefully, placing all ingredients except honey and nuts in bread machine pan in order specified by owner's manual. Program dough cycle setting; press start.

2. Roll dough into 20×6-inch rectangle. Cut lengthwise into 5 equal strips. On greased baking sheet, twist strips and wind around into a loose spiral. Cover and let rise in warm place 45 minutes or until doubled.

3. Preheat oven to 375°F. Drizzle honey over dough; sprinkle with nuts. Bake 25 to 30 minutes or until evenly browned. Remove from baking sheet; cool on wire rack. *Makes 1 coffee cake*

Poppy Seed Braid

INGREDIENTS

⅓ cup water
1 teaspoon salt
2 eggs
2 tablespoons butter or margarine, softened
2¼ cups all-purpose flour
2 tablespoons sugar
2 teaspoons active dry yeast
1 egg white
1 tablespoon poppy seeds

1. Measure carefully, placing all ingredients except egg white and poppy seeds in bread machine pan in order specified by owner's manual. Program dough cycle setting; press start.

2. Divide dough into 3 equal pieces. Shape each piece into 20-inch-long rope. Braid strands loosely together. Tuck ends under and pinch to seal. Place on greased baking sheet. Cover and let rise in warm place 1½ hours or until doubled.

3. Preheat oven to 375°F. Beat egg white with fork and brush over braid. Sprinkle poppy seeds over braid. Bake 25 to 30 minutes or until golden and loaf sounds hollow when tapped. Remove braid from baking sheet; cool on wire rack. *Makes 1 loaf*

Cheddar Pepper Bread

INGREDIENTS

Basic Yeast Bread (page 14)
1 cup (4 ounces) cubed sharp Cheddar cheese
⅓ cup chopped green bell pepper
⅓ cup chopped red bell pepper
¼ cup chopped onion
1 egg
1 tablespoon water
Coarse salt (optional)

1. Prepare Basic Yeast Bread dough as instructed, adding cheese, bell peppers and onion after end of first kneading cycle.

2. Grease baking sheet; set aside. Turn out dough onto lightly floured surface. Cover with clean towel; let rest 5 minutes.

3. Shape dough into a ball. Place on prepared baking sheet. Flatten dough to about 2 inches thick. Cover with towel; let rise in warm place 45 minutes.

4. Beat egg with 1 tablespoon water in small bowl. Lightly brush top and side of dough with egg mixture. Sprinkle top with coarse salt, if desired.

5. Preheat oven to 375°F. Bake 30 minutes or until golden brown. Immediately remove to wire rack; cool. *Makes 1 loaf*

Cheddar Pepper Bread

Whole Wheat Carrot Bread

INGREDIENTS

2 tablespoons oil
2 tablespoons honey
½ cup cottage cheese
1 cup grated carrots
1½ teaspoons dried dill weed
½ teaspoon dried mustard
1 teaspoon grated orange zest
1 teaspoon salt
⅔ cup whole wheat flour
1⅓ cups bread flour
1½ teaspoons RED STAR® Active Dry Yeast or QUICK•RISE™ Yeast

Bread Machine Method
Select Red Star® Active Dry Yeast or Quick•Rise™ Yeast as is appropriate for your automatic bread machine. All ingredients should be at room temperature. Place ingredients into pan in order suggested by machine's manual.

Rising, Shaping and Baking
Turn dough onto lightly floured surface; punch down to remove air bubbles. Roll or pat into 10×4-inch rectangle. Starting with shorter side, roll up tightly, pressing dough into roll. Pinch edges and ends to seal. Place in greased 8×4-inch loaf pan. Cover; let rise until indentation remains after touching. Bake in preheated 375°F oven approximately 30 minutes. Remove from pan; cool. *Makes 1 loaf*

Spinach-Feta-Wild Rice Bread

INGREDIENTS

- ¾ cup water
- 2 tablespoons honey
- 2 ounces frozen chopped spinach, thawed and squeezed dry
- 2½ cups bread flour
- ½ cup whole wheat flour
- ¾ teaspoon salt
- 1 tablespoon dried Italian seasoning
- 1 cup cooked wild rice
- 2 ounces crumbled feta cheese
- 2 teaspoons active dry yeast (not rapid rise)

1. Measure carefully, placing all ingredients in bread machine pan in order specified by owner's manual.

2. Turn out dough onto lightly floured surface; shape into 2 to 3 baguettes. Place on prepared baking sheet; cover and let rise in warm place 45 minutes or until doubled.

3. Bake in preheated 375°F oven 20 to 25 minutes or until browned and sounds hollow when lightly tapped. *Makes 2 to 3 baguettes*

Favorite recipe from *Minnesota Cultivated Wild Rice Council*

Let's Make Pizza

Fresh Tomato Pizza

INGREDIENTS

New York-Style Pizza Crust (page 91)
1 to 1¼ pounds ripe tomatoes, cored
1 tablespoon olive oil
3 to 4 cloves garlic, minced
½ cup (2 ounces) shredded Monterey Jack cheese or part-skim mozzarella cheese
2 tablespoons grated Parmesan cheese
Cracked black pepper
10 to 12 fresh basil leaves

1. Prepare New York-Style Pizza Crust. Preheat oven to 500°F.

2. Slice tomatoes and place between double layers of paper towels. Press gently to remove juice.

3. Combine oil and garlic in small bowl. Brush oil mixture over entire surface of prepared crust. Pierce surface with fork 12 to14 times. Sprinkle with Monterey Jack cheese leaving 1-inch border. Bake 3 to 4 minutes or until crust is light golden and cheese is melted.

4. Arrange tomato slices over cheese. Sprinkle with Parmesan cheese and pepper. Bake 4 to 6 minutes or until crust is dark golden. Cut into 8 wedges. Top with whole or slivered basil leaves. *Makes 4 servings*

Fresh Tomato Pizza

Barbecue Chicken Pizza

INGREDIENTS

New York-Style Pizza Crust (page 91)
6 ounces boneless skinless chicken breasts
2 teaspoons olive oil
¼ to ⅓ cup barbecue sauce
½ medium red onion, thinly sliced
½ green bell pepper, diced
½ cup (2 ounces) shredded reduced-fat Monterey Jack cheese
¼ cup fresh cilantro leaves

1. Prepare New York-Style Pizza Crust. Preheat oven to 500°F.

2. Slice chicken into ¼-inch-thick strips. Bring 4 cups water to a boil in large saucepan over high heat. Stir in chicken; cover and remove from heat. Let stand 3 to 4 minutes or until chicken is no longer pink in center. Drain; set aside.

3. Brush oil evenly over prepared crust. Spread barbecue sauce over crust leaving 1-inch border. Arrange onions over sauce. Top with chicken, bell peppers and cheese. Bake 10 minutes or until crust is dark golden brown. Sprinkle with cilantro and cut into 8 wedges.

Makes 4 servings

Barbecue Chicken Pizza

Italian Covered Deep Dish Pizza

INGREDIENTS

Herbed Pizza Crust (page 89)
2 cups (16 ounces) part-skim ricotta cheese
1 tablespoon cornstarch
1 teaspoon *each* dried basil and dried oregano
½ teaspoon ground black pepper
1 jar (7 ounces) roasted red peppers, drained, chopped, divided
1 clove garlic
1 bag (10 ounces) washed fresh spinach leaves
¼ pound thinly sliced lean ham
6 tablespoons (2½ ounces) shredded Romano cheese
½ teaspoon olive oil

1. Prepare Herbed Pizza Crust as directed through step 1. Preheat oven to 500°F.

2. Combine ricotta, cornstarch, basil, oregano and pepper in large bowl; set aside. Place ½ cup roasted peppers and garlic in food processor or blender; process until puréed.

3. Remove stems from spinach leaves. Place half the spinach and 1 tablespoon water in large skillet or Dutch oven over medium-high heat. Cover and cook 1 minute. Turn spinach and cook until just wilted. Drain on paper towels. Repeat with remaining spinach. Top spinach with paper towels; press gently to remove moisture.

4. Knead dough on lightly floured surface 2 minutes or until smooth. Roll into log. Cut off ⅓ of dough; cover and set aside. Roll remaining ⅔ of dough into 15-inch disk, following directions in step 2 of Herbed Pizza Crust recipe. Spray 14-inch deep-dish pizza pan with nonstick cooking spray. Place dough in pan, easing into edges and up sides; let excess dough hang over lip of pan.

5. Cover bottom with ham. Spread evenly with cheese mixture. Cover with spinach. Top with remaining chopped red peppers. Roll remaining dough to 12- to 13-inch round. Place over filling. Brush ½ inch of edge with water. Fold overhanging crust over top and press gently to seal. Bake 10 to 12 minutes, until crust is golden. Spread puréed roasted peppers over center of top crust. Sprinkle with Romano. Bake 6 to 8 minutes, until crust is deep golden on top and crisp on bottom. Brush edge of crust with olive oil.

Makes 8 servings

Italian Covered Deep Dish Pizza

Mu Shu Pork Calzones

INGREDIENTS

New York-Style Pizza Crust (page 91)
4 dry shiitake mushrooms (optional)
Nonstick cooking spray
¼ cup fat-free egg substitute
1 boneless pork chop (5 to 6 ounces), fat trimmed and cut into thin slices
½ to 1 jalapeño pepper,* seeded and minced (optional)
1 tablespoon minced ginger
3 cloves garlic, minced
2 cups very thinly sliced Napa cabbage
⅓ cup thinly sliced green onions
2 tablespoons hoisin sauce
1 tablespoon dark sesame oil
1 teaspoon canola oil

*Jalapeño peppers can sting and irritate the skin; wear rubber gloves when handling peppers and do not touch eyes. Wash hands after handling.

1. Prepare New York-Style Pizza Crust as directed through step 1. Preheat oven to 500°F.

2. Cover mushrooms with hot water in small bowl; let stand 15 minutes or until caps are tender. Drain; squeeze water from mushrooms. Cut out and discard tough stems. Thinly slice caps; set aside.

3. Spray large skillet generously with cooking spray. Heat over medium-high heat until hot. Add egg substitute; cover and cook 2 minutes or until set on top. Loosen egg from skillet and transfer to plate. When egg is cool enough to handle, roll up and slice into ¼-inch-wide strips; set aside.

4. Spray same large skillet with nonstick cooking spray. Heat over medium-high heat until hot. Add pork, jalapeño pepper, ginger and garlic. Cook and stir about 2 minutes or until pork is no longer pink in center. Add cabbage and green onions; cook and stir 1½ to 2 minutes or until cabbage is wilted. Spoon mixture into medium bowl and gently stir in mushroom and egg strips; set aside.

5. Combine hoisin and sesame oil in small bowl.

6. Divide dough in half. On lightly floured surface, roll each half into 9- to 10-inch round. Cut each round in half. Brush half of each dough piece with about 1 teaspoon hoisin mixture leaving ½-inch border. Spoon pork mixture over top. Drizzle remaining hoisin mixture evenly over pork mixture (about 1 teaspoon each). Brush edges with water. Fold dough over filling and press edges together. Seal with tines of fork. Place on lightly oiled baking sheet. Brush calzones with canola oil. Bake 6 to 7 minutes or until light golden brown. *Makes 4 servings*

Corn and Tomato Pizza

INGREDIENTS

Cornmeal Crust (page 90)
1½ cups frozen corn, thawed
1½ cups seeded and chopped plum tomatoes
¼ cup chopped fresh basil
3 cloves garlic, minced
1 teaspoon dried oregano leaves
½ teaspoon coarse ground black pepper
2 tablespoons Dijon mustard (optional)
1 cup (4 ounces) shredded reduced-fat part-skim mozzarella cheese
2 tablespoons grated Parmesan cheese

1. Prepare Cornmeal Crust. Preheat oven to 450°F.

2. Combine corn, tomatoes, basil, garlic, oregano and pepper in medium bowl.

3. Spread mustard over prepared crust, if desired. Sprinkle crust with mozzarella cheese; top with corn mixture and Parmesan cheese. Bake 18 to 20 minutes or until crust is golden brown and cheese is melted. Cut into 8 wedges. *Makes 8 servings*

Mexican Deep Dish Pizza

INGREDIENTS

Thick Pizza Crust (page 88)
Nonstick cooking spray
½ small onion, diced
1 teaspoon chili powder
½ teaspoon ground cumin
¼ teaspoon ground cinnamon
1 can (15 ounces) 50%-less-sodium black beans, rinsed and drained
½ can (4 ounces) diced green chilies (optional)
Cornmeal
1 cup (4 ounces) shredded reduced-fat Cheddar cheese or reduced-fat Monterey Jack cheese
¾ cup diced tomatoes
½ cup frozen whole kernel corn, thawed
½ green bell pepper, diced
½ can (2¼ ounces) sliced ripe black olives, drained
½ teaspoon olive oil
Salsa (optional)
Reduced-fat sour cream (optional)

1. Prepare Thick Pizza Crust through step 1. Preheat oven to 500°F.

2. Spray 2- to 3-quart saucepan with cooking spray. Place over medium heat. Add onion, chili powder, cumin, cinnamon and 1 tablespoon water; stir. Cover and cook 3 to 4 minutes or until onion is crisp-tender. Stir in beans and chilies, if desired. Transfer ½ of the bean mixture to food processor or blender; process until almost smooth.

3. Spray 14-inch deep-dish pizza pan with nonstick cooking spray; sprinkle with cornmeal. Press dough gently into bottom and up side of pan. Cover with plastic wrap and let stand in warm place 15 to 20 minutes or until puffy. Bake 5 to 7 minutes or until dry and firm on top.

4. Spread puréed bean mixture over crust up to thick edge. Top with half the cheese, remaining bean mixture, tomatoes, corn, bell pepper and olives. Top with remaining cheese. Bake 10 to 12 minutes more or until crust is deep golden. Brush crust edges with olive oil. Cut into 8 wedges. Serve with salsa and sour cream, if desired.

Makes 4 servings

Mexican Deep Dish Pizza

Spinach-Basil Pesto Pizzas with Sun-Dried Tomatoes and Roquefort

INGREDIENTS

Whole Wheat Crust (page 90)
1 cup packed fresh spinach
1 cup packed fresh basil
4 cloves garlic
2 tablespoons grated Parmesan cheese
2 tablespoons pine nuts
2 tablespoons fresh lemon juice
1 tablespoon olive oil
½ cup sun-dried tomatoes
½ cup crumbled Roquefort cheese

1. Prepare dough for Whole Wheat Crust through step 1.

2. Combine spinach, basil, garlic, Parmesan cheese and pine nuts in food processor or blender; process until finely chopped. With motor running, gradually add lemon juice and oil; process until smooth.

3. Bring sun-dried tomatoes and enough water to cover to a boil in small saucepan over medium-high heat. Remove from heat. Cover and let stand 5 to 10 minutes or until tomatoes are softened. Drain and pat dry with paper towels. Cut tomatoes into ¼-inch strips.

4. Preheat oven to 450°F.

5. Cut dough into 20 equal portions. Shape dough into 2½-inch rounds, about ¼-inch thick. Top each round with 1 teaspoon pesto, 3 to 4 tomato strips and about 1 teaspoon Roquefort cheese. Place on baking sheet and bake 10 to 12 minutes or until crust is golden brown and cheese is melted.

Makes 10 appetizer servings

Spinach-Basil Pesto Pizzas with Sun-Dried Tomatoes and Roquefort

Artichoke Heart, Olive and Goat Cheese Pizza

INGREDIENTS

New York-Style Pizza Crust (page 91)
2 teaspoons olive oil
2 teaspoons minced fresh rosemary leaves *or* 1 teaspoon dried rosemary leaves
3 cloves garlic, minced
½ cup (2 ounces) shredded reduced-fat Monterey Jack cheese, divided
1 jar (14 ounces) water-packed artichoke hearts, drained
3 slices oil-packed sun-dried tomatoes, drained
2½ ounces soft ripe goat cheese such as Montrachet, sliced or crumbled
10 kalamata olives, pitted, halved (about ¼ cup)

1. Prepare New York-Style Pizza Crust. Preheat oven to 500°F.

2. Brush surface with olive oil. Sprinkle with rosemary and garlic and brush again to coat with oil. Bake about 4 minutes or until crust begins to turn golden.

3. Sprinkle with ¼ cup Monterey Jack cheese, leaving 1-inch border. Top with artichokes, tomatoes, goat cheese and olives. Sprinkle with remaining ¼ cup Monterey Jack cheese. Return to oven and bake 3 to 4 minutes more or until crust is deep golden and Monterey Jack cheese is melted. Cut into 8 wedges. *Makes 4 servings*

Artichoke Heart, Olive and Goat Cheese Pizza

Shrimp and Pineapple Pizza

INGREDIENTS

New York-Style Pizza Crust (page 91)
1 tablespoon olive oil
½ cup shredded Monterey Jack cheese or part-skim mozzarella cheese
6 ounces cooked shrimp
1 can (8 ounces) chunk pineapple, drained
½ green bell pepper, diced
3 tablespoons shredded Parmesan cheese
¼ cup fresh cilantro leaves
Crushed red pepper

1. Prepare New York-Style Pizza Crust. Preheat oven to 500°F.

2. Brush prepared crust with olive oil; sprinkle with Monterey Jack cheese. Top with shrimp, pineapple, bell pepper and Parmesan cheese.

3. Bake about 8 minutes or until crust is deep golden and cheese is melted. Sprinkle with cilantro and red pepper. Cut into 8 wedges.

Makes 4 servings

Shrimp and Pineapple Pizza

Pesto, Tomato and Pepper Pizza

INGREDIENTS

Black Pepper Pizza Crust (page 88)
8 ounces roma tomatoes, cored
⅓ cup basil pesto
1 large yellow bell pepper, cut into rings
1 tablespoon pine nuts
Cracked black pepper
½ teaspoon olive oil

1. Prepare Black Pepper Pizza Crust. Preheat oven to 500°F.

2. Slice tomatoes into ¼-inch-thick rounds. Place slices in single layer between double layers of paper towels. Press gently to remove juice. Set aside.

3. Spread pesto over prepared crust leaving ½- to 1-inch border. Place bell pepper slices over pesto. Arrange tomato slices over peppers, tucking some edges under peppers. Sprinkle with pine nuts and black pepper. Bake 10 to 12 minutes or until crust is deep golden. Slide pizza onto cutting board. Brush edge of crust with olive oil. Cut into 8 wedges.

Makes 4 servings

Pesto, Tomato and Pepper Pizza

Roasted Red Pepper, Eggplant, Goat Cheese and Olive Pizza

INGREDIENTS

Nonstick cooking spray
1 small eggplant, cut into ¼-inch-thick slices
1 tablespoon olive oil
¼ cup finely chopped onion
1 tablespoon minced fresh rosemary leaves *or* 2 teaspoons dried rosemary
3 large cloves garlic, minced
½ cup roasted red pepper strips
1 (12-inch) round prepared Italian bread shell or New York-Style Pizza Crust (page 91)
2 ounces goat cheese, crumbled
6 kalamata olives, pitted and halved
Coarse ground black pepper

1. Preheat oven to 500°F. Spray baking sheet with cooking spray. Place eggplant slices on baking sheet; spray with cooking spray. Bake 8 to 10 minutes or until light golden. Turn slices over and bake 6 to 8 minutes more or until slices are golden and very tender. Set aside.

2. Meanwhile, in small skillet over medium heat combine oil, onion, rosemary and garlic. Cook and stir 3 to 4 minutes or until onion is translucent. Set aside.

3. Place red peppers in food processor or blender; process until smooth. Set aside.

4. Bake bread shell 3 to 4 minutes or until top is crisp and beginning to brown. Spread puréed red peppers evenly over pizza leaving 1-inch border. Arrange eggplant over top, slightly overlapping slices. Spoon or brush onion mixture over eggplant. Top with cheese, olives and black pepper. Bake 3 to 5 minutes more or until crust is deep golden.

Makes 4 servings

Roasted Red Pepper, Eggplant, Goat Cheese and Olive Pizza

Spicy Thai Pizza

INGREDIENTS

Whole Wheat Crust (page 90)
⅓ cup rice wine vinegar
3 tablespoons low-sodium soy sauce
3 tablespoons reduced-fat chunky peanut butter
2 tablespoons lime juice
3 cloves garlic, minced
1 tablespoon minced fresh ginger
¼ teaspoon black pepper
¼ teaspoon crushed red pepper
½ pound medium shrimp, peeled
1 tablespoon cornstarch
⅓ cup water
1 cup (4 ounces) shredded part-skim mozzarella cheese
½ cup chopped red bell pepper
½ cup sliced baby corn
¼ cup sliced green onions
2 tablespoons chopped fresh cilantro

1. Prepare Whole Wheat Crust. Preheat oven to 450°F.

2. Combine vinegar, soy sauce, peanut butter, lime juice, garlic, ginger, black pepper and crushed red pepper in 2-cup glass measure; stir to combine.

3. Spray large skillet with nonstick cooking spray. Heat over medium-high heat until hot. Add shrimp; cook and stir 5 to 7 minutes or until shrimp turn pink and opaque. Transfer shrimp to small bowl.

4. Add vinegar mixture to same skillet; bring to a boil. Reduce heat to medium-low and simmer 3 to 4 minutes or until slightly thickened.

5. Combine cornstarch and water in small bowl; stir until smooth. Add cornstarch mixture to vinegar mixture in skillet; cook and stir about 5 minutes or until thickened. Remove from heat.

6. Sprinkle cheese over dough. Spread vinegar mixture evenly over cheese. Top with shrimp, bell pepper, baby corn and green onions.

7. Bake 18 to 20 minutes or until crust is golden brown and cheese is melted. Sprinkle with cilantro. *Makes 8 servings*

Spicy Thai Pizza

Black Pepper Pizza Crust

INGREDIENTS

⅔ cup warm water, 110° to 115°F
½ teaspoon salt
2¼ cups all-purpose or bread flour
1 teaspoon sugar
½ teaspoon black pepper
2 teaspoons active dry yeast
1 tablespoon cornmeal (optional)

1. Measure carefully, placing all ingredients except cornmeal in bread machine pan in order specified by owner's manual. Program dough cycle setting; press start. Remove dough from bread machine pan; let rest 2 to 3 minutes.

2. Pat and gently stretch dough from edges until dough seems to not stretch anymore. Let rest 2 to 3 minutes more. Continue patting and stretching until dough is 12 to 14 inches in diameter. Spray 12- to 14-inch pizza pan with cooking spray; sprinkle with cornmeal, if desired. Press dough into pan.

3. Preheat oven to 500°F. Follow topping and baking directions for individual recipes, baking pizza on bottom rack of oven.

Makes 1 thin 14-inch crust (4 servings)

Thick Pizza Crust

INGREDIENTS

¾ cup warm water, 110° to 115°F
½ teaspoon salt
2½ cups all-purpose or bread flour
1 teaspoon sugar
2 teaspoons active dry yeast
1 tablespoon cornmeal (optional)

1. Measure carefully, placing all ingredients except cornmeal in bread machine pan in order specified by owner's manual. Program dough cycle setting; press start. Remove dough from bread machine pan; let rest 2 to 3 minutes.

2. Pat and gently stretch dough from edges until dough seems to not

stretch anymore. Let rest 2 to 3 minutes more. Continue patting and stretching until dough is 12 to 14 inches in diameter. Spray 12- to 14-inch pizza pan with nonstick cooking spray; sprinkle with cornmeal, if desired. Press into pan. Cover with towel and let stand in warm place 10 to 20 minutes or until slightly puffed

3. Position oven rack in lowest position. Preheat oven to 500°F. Prick crust with fork at 2-inch intervals. Bake 4 to 5 minutes or until top is dry but not yet golden. Remove from oven. Follow topping and baking directions for individual recipes. *Makes 1 thick 12-inch crust or 1 medium-thick 14-inch crust (4 servings)*

Herbed Pizza Crust

INGREDIENTS

⅔ cup warm water, 110° to 115°F
½ teaspoon salt
2¼ cups all-purpose or bread flour
1 teaspoon sugar
1 teaspoon dried rosemary leaves
½ teaspoon dried oregano leaves
¼ teaspoon ground black pepper
¼ teaspoon dried thyme leaves
2 teaspoons active dry yeast
1 tablespoon cornmeal (optional)

1. Measure carefully, placing all ingredients except cornmeal in bread machine pan in order specified by owner's manual. Program dough cycle setting; press start. Remove dough from bread machine pan; let rest 2 to 3 minutes.

2. Pat and gently stretch dough from edges until dough seems to not stretch anymore. Let rest 2 to 3 minutes more. Continue patting and stretching until dough is 12 to 14 inches in diameter. Spray 12- to 14-inch pizza pan with cooking spray; sprinkle with cornmeal, if desired. Press dough into pan. Cover with towel and let stand in warm place 10 to 20 minutes or until slightly puffed.

3. Position oven rack in lowest position. Preheat oven to 500°F. Prick crust with fork at 2-inch intervals. Bake 4 to 5 minutes or until top is dry but not yet golden. Remove from oven. Follow topping and baking directions for individual recipes. *Makes 1 thick 12-inch crust or 1 medium-thick 14-inch crust*

Cornmeal Crust

INGREDIENTS

1 cup warm water, 110° to 115°F
¼ teaspoon salt (optional)
2½ cups all-purpose flour, divided
1 cup plus 1 tablespoon cornmeal, divided
2 tablespoons sugar or honey
2 teaspoons active dry yeast

1. Measure carefully, placing all ingredients except 1 tablespoon cornmeal in bread machine pan in order specified by owner's manual. Program basic dough cycle setting; press start. Remove dough from bread machine pan; let rest 2 to 3 minutes.

2. Pat and gently stretch dough into 14- to 15-inch circle. Spray 14-inch pizza pan with nonstick cooking spray; sprinkle with remaining 1 tablespoon cornmeal. Press dough into pan.

3. Follow topping and baking directions for individual recipes.

Makes 1 thick 14-inch crust (8 servings)

Whole Wheat Crust

INGREDIENTS

1¼ cups warm water, 110° to 115°F
¼ teaspoon salt (optional)
2 tablespoons honey or sugar
2 to 2½ cups all-purpose flour, divided
1 cup whole wheat flour
2 teaspoons active dry yeast
1 tablespoon cornmeal

1. Measure carefully, placing all ingredients except cornmeal in bread machine pan in order specified by owner's manual. Program dough cycle setting; press start. Remove dough from bread machine pan; let rest 2 to 3 minutes.

2. Pat and gently stretch dough into 14- to 15-inch circle. Spray 14-inch pizza pan with nonstick cooking spray; sprinkle with cornmeal, if desired. Press dough into pan.

3. Follow topping and baking directions for individual recipes.

Makes 1 thick 14-inch crust (8 servings)

New York-Style Pizza Crust

INGREDIENTS

⅔ cup warm water, 110° to 115°F
½ teaspoon salt
2¼ cups all-purpose or bread flour
1 teaspoon sugar
2 teaspoons active dry yeast
1 tablespoon cornmeal (optional)

1. Measure carefully, placing all ingredients except cornmeal in bread machine pan in order specified by owner's manual. Program dough cycle setting; press start. Remove dough from bread machine pan; let rest 2 to 3 minutes.

2. Pat and gently stretch dough from edges until dough seems to not stretch anymore. Let rest 2 to 3 minutes more. Continue patting and stretching until dough is 12 to 14 inches in diameter. Spray 12- to 14-inch pizza pan with cooking spray; sprinkle with cornmeal, if desired. Press dough into pan.

3. Preheat oven to 500°F. Follow topping and baking directions for individual recipes, baking pizza on bottom rack of oven.

Makes 1 thin 14-inch crust (4 servings)

INDEX

A

Apricot Holiday Bread, 14
Artichoke Heart, Olive and Goat Cheese Pizza, 78

B

Bagels, 58
Barbecue Chicken Pizza, 68
Basic Yeast Bread, 14
Black Pepper Pizza Crust, 88
Bread Flour
  Bagels, 58
  Breadsticks, 52
  Carrot-Raisin-Nut Bread, 10
  Cherry Granola Bread, 30
  Cinnamon Pear Rolls, 57
  Cracked Wheat Bread, 27
  Dakota Bread, 32
  Dilled Buttermilk Bread, 34
  German Rye Beer Bread, 30
  Honey of a Whole Wheat Bread, 16
  Jalapeño Cheese Bread, 17
  Jalapeño Corn Bread, 22
  Maple-Walnut Bread, 24
  Multigrain Bread, 36
  Oatmeal-Raisin Bread, 20
  Parmesan and Herb Bread, 26
  Pepper Sweet Corn Bread, 33
  Potato Bread, 28
  Sun-Dried Tomato and Basil Bread, 12
  Whole Wheat Carrot Bread, 64
Breads, Savory
  Cheddar Pepper Bread, 62
  Dilled Buttermilk Bread, 34
  Gannat (French Cheese Bread), 16
  German Rye Beer Bread, 30
  Greek Flat Breads, 54
  Italian Pan Rolls, 60
  Jalapeño Cheese Bread, 17
  Jalapeño Corn Bread, 22
  Parmesan and Herb Bread, 26
  Peppered Cheese Baguettes, 48
  Pepper Sweet Corn Bread, 33
  Savory Pull-Apart Loaves, 50
  Spinach-Feta-Wild Rice Bread, 65
  Sun-Dried Tomato and Basil Bread, 12
Breads, Sweet
  Apricot Holiday Bread, 14
  Caramel Sticky Buns, 44
  Carrot-Raisin-Nut Bread, 10
  Cherry Granola Bread, 30
  Chocolate Rolls, 46
  Cinnamon Pear Rolls, 57
  Honey Pecan Coffee Cake, 60
  Hot Cross Buns, 40
  Maple-Walnut Bread, 24
  Oatmeal-Raisin Bread, 20
  Old-Fashioned Cinnamon Braid, 42
  Orange Breakfast Loaf, 18
  Saint Lucia Crown, 45
Breadsticks, 52
Buttery Pan Rolls, 56

C

Caramel Sticky Buns, 44
Caramel Topping, 44
Carrot-Raisin-Nut Bread, 10
Cheddar Pepper Bread, 62
Cherry Granola Bread, 30
Chocolate Rolls, 46
Cinnamon Pear Rolls, 57
Cinnamon Sugar Filling, 42
Coffee Cakes
  Honey Pecan Coffee Cake, 60
  Saint Lucia Crown, 45
Corn and Tomato Pizza, 73
Cornmeal Crust, 91
Cracked Wheat Bread, 27
Crusty Rye Bread, 18

D

Dakota Bread, 32
Dilled Buttermilk Bread, 34

F
Fresh Tomato Pizza, 66
Fruit (*see also* Raisins)
Apricot Holiday Bread, 14
Cinnamon Pear Rolls, 57
Orange Breakfast Loaf, 18
Pesto, Tomato and Pepper Pizza, 82

G
Gannat (French Cheese Bread), 16
German Rye Beer Bread, 30
Glaze, 42
Greek Flat Breads, 54

H
Herbed Pizza Crust, 89
Honey of a Whole Wheat Bread, 16
Honey Pecan Coffee Cake, 60
Honey Wheat Bread, 38
Hot Cross Buns, 40

I
Italian Covered Deep Dish Pizza, 70
Italian Pan Rolls, 60

J
Jalapeño Cheese Bread, 17
Jalapeño Corn Bread, 22

L
Light Rye Rolls, 49

M
Maple-Walnut Bread, 24
Mexican Deep Dish Pizza, 74
Multigrain Bread, 36
Mu Shu Pork Calzones, 72

N
New York-Style Pizza Crust, 91
Nuts
Apricot Holiday Bread, 14
Carrot-Raisin-Nut Bread, 10
Honey Pecan Coffee Cake, 60
Maple-Walnut Bread, 24
Saint Lucia Crown, 45

O
Oatmeal-Raisin Bread, 20
Old-Fashioned Cinnamon Braid, 42
Old-Fashioned Hearth Bread, 20
Orange Breakfast Loaf, 18

P
Parmesan and Herb Bread, 26
Peppered Cheese Baguettes, 48
Pepper Sweet Corn Bread, 33
Pesto, Tomato and Pepper Pizza, 82
Pizza Crusts
Black Pepper Pizza Crust, 88
Cornmeal Crust, 90
Herbed Pizza Crust, 89
New York-Style Pizza Crust, 91
Thick Pizza Crust, 88
Whole Wheat Crust, 90
Poppy Seed Braid, 61
Potato Bread, 28

R
Raisins
Carrot-Raisin-Nut Bread, 10
Cinnamon Pear Rolls, 57
Hot Cross Buns, 40
Oatmeal-Raisin Bread, 20
Saint Lucia Crown, 45
Roasted Red Pepper, Eggplant, Goat Cheese and Olive Pizza, 84
Rolls
Buttery Pan Rolls, 56
Caramel Sticky Buns, 44
Chocolate Rolls, 46
Cinnamon Pear Rolls, 57
Hot Cross Buns, 40
Italian Pan Rolls, 60
Light Rye Rolls, 49
Rye Flour
Crusty Rye Bread, 18
German Rye Beer Bread, 30
Light Rye Rolls, 49

S
Saint Lucia Crown, 45
Sandwich Breads
Basic Yeast Bread, 14
Cracked Wheat Bread, 27
Crusty Rye Bread, 18
Dakota Bread, 32
Honey of a Whole Wheat Bread, 16
Honey Wheat Bread, 38
Multigrain Bread, 36
Old-Fashioned Hearth Bread, 20
Potato Bread, 28
Savory Pull-Apart Loaves, 50
Shrimp and Pineapple Pizza, 80
Spicy Thai Pizza, 86
Spinach-Basil Pesto Pizzas with Sun-Dried Tomatoes and Roquefort, 76
Spinach-Feta-Wild Rice Bread, 65
Sugar Icing, 45
Sun-Dried Tomato and Basil Bread, 12

T
Thick Pizza Crust, 88

W
Whole Wheat Carrot Bread, 64
Whole Wheat Crust, 90
Whole Wheat Flour
Carrot-Raisin-Nut Bread, 10
Cherry Granola Bread, 30
Dakota Bread, 32
Honey of a Whole Wheat Bread, 16
Honey Wheat Bread, 38
Maple-Walnut Bread, 24
Orange Breakfast Loaf, 18
Spinach-Feta-Wild Rice Bread, 65
Sun-Dried Tomato and Basil Bread, 12
Whole Wheat Carrot Bread, 64
Whole Wheat Crust, 90

ACKNOWLEDGMENTS

The publisher would like to thank the companies and organizations listed below for the use of their recipes and photographs in this publication.

Cherry Marketing Institute, Inc.

Minnesota Cultivated Wild Rice Council

North Dakota Wheat Commission

RED STAR® Yeast & Products,
a Division of Universal Foods Corporation